BBC CHILDREN'S BOOKS

UK | USA | Canada | Ireland | Australia
India | New Zealand | South Africa

BBC Children's Books are published by Puffin Books,
part of the Penguin Random House group of companies
whose addresses can be found at global.penguinrandomhouse.com.
www.penguin.co.uk   www.puffin.co.uk   www.ladybird.co.uk

Penguin
Random House
UK

First published 2016
002

Written by Kevin Pettman
Copyright © BBC Worldwide Limited, 2016

BBC and Top Gear (word marks and logos) are trade marks of the British
Broadcasting Corporation and are used under licence.
Top Gear logo TM & © BBC 2005.
BBC logo TM & © BBC 1996.

The moral right of the author and copyright holders has been asserted

Printed in China

A CIP catalogue record for this book is available from the British Library

ISBN: 978–1–405–92894–6

All correspondence to:
BBC Children's Books
Penguin Random House Children's
80 Strand, London WC2R 0RL

BBC TopGear

100

FASTESTCARS

PUFFIN

Contents

Introduction

*T*op *Gear* loves driving cars. Very often, we get to drive very fast cars very quickly on the *Top Gear* track. Which means we know a thing or six about speed, acceleration, power and why the hairs on the back of your neck stand up at the mere sight of Ferraris, McLarens, Lamborghinis and Aston Martins.

Top Gear 100 Fastest Cars is packed with lots (well, 100, to be precise) of speed machines, but they're not all 200-mph, £1 million supercars. Some of them you'll never have heard of, some are old, some are new, some have three wheels, some have six … and some haven't really been built yet.

This book isn't just about top speeds, zero to 60 mph, or whether the Stig can drive a car sideways in a cloud of tyre smoke. It's about the thrill of how these cars make you feel. Each one is cool in its own way, and we'll tell you why.

The only thing we can't actually tell you, though, is *why* the hairs on your neck stand up — something to do with terminal velocity and eating Stilton cheese, perhaps?

Stig Factor: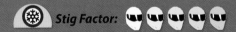

No car in this book is completely uncool — we know you don't want to see a 1999 Nissan Micra, for example. The Stig rates each one using his Stig Factor scale, which means if a car has five helmets it's seriously hot. By which he means cool — we think!

01

Please don't complain that we've already made a mistake with the very first car – the stats below are correct. This thumping Fiat 500 *does* have 187 brake horsepower (bhp), it *does* clock 60 mph in under six seconds and the basic model *will* cost you a tenner short of £33,000.

We know that's ridiculous, but an Abarth hot hatch *should* be ridiculous and make your hands shake just a little every time you turn the key. The rear seats, stereo, air con, satnav and cupholders have all been scrapped from this lightweight lunatic, so the Biposto is definitely more of a track-day blaster than a weekly Waitrose runner.

 Power: *187 bhp*

 0–60 mph: *5.9 seconds*

 Top Speed: *143 mph*

 Price: *£32,990*

 Stig Factor:

02 Alfa Romeo 4C

"**P**retty" is a good word to describe the 4C. It looks pretty, it's pretty cool, pretty economical, pretty good to drive and pretty quick. Actually, it's pretty bloomin' quick with a four-cylinder, turbocharged 1.7-litre engine that hits 60 in sub five and has a carbon chassis that's more agile than a Border collie on *Britain's Got Talent*.

Any drawbacks? A couple. The 4c is nearly as wide as a Discovery and the engine and road noise makes you want to stick your fingers in your ears, which is not a good idea in the outside lane on the M1. Our advice is to put some ear defenders on before you get behind the wheel of this awesome Alfa, but then that wouldn't be a very pretty look!

Power: 240 bhp

0–60 mph: 4.5 seconds

Top Speed: 160 mph

Price: £51,265

Stig Factor:

ES·992VB

13

03 *Alfa Romeo Giulia*

It seems like Alfa Romeo has been teasing petrolheads with pictures of the Giulia since about 1992. When the real thing finally rocked up at the 2016 Geneva International Motor Show, those same fans continued drooling down their Hypercolor T-shirts.

The Italians hope this striking saloon will give the smug-looking Germans, with their 3 series and A4s, a run for their euros. But it might take the much-hyped Quadrifoglio version — a fire-breathing 500-bhp, V6 monster — to really scare the opposition. It certainly looks scary, which will put a smile on petrolheads' faces.

 Power: *503 bhp (petrol)*

 0–60 mph: *3.9 seconds*

 Top Speed: *190 mph*

 Price: *£60,000 approx*

Stig Factor:

Scaffold doesn't have a reputation for moving very fast, but head to Somerset and you could see it flash past your eyes in the, er, blink of an eye. You see, Somerset is where the crazy Ariel guys create the frighteningly fast Atom – a high-tech, high-speed go-cart held together by strips of scaffold. Well, technically it's a hand-welded tubular chassis, but you know what we mean.

With the help of a few spanners and a shiny supercharger, the Atom 3.5R squeezes a mighty 350 bhp from its 2.0-litre Honda Civic Type R engine, making it one of the fastest cars ever to rocket round the *Top Gear* track!

 Power: *350 bhp*

 0–60 mph: *2.5 seconds*

 Top Speed: *155 mph*

 Price: *£64,800*

 Stig Factor:

04

Before 2015, the best place to blast a car made by Ariel was on the track. Or an empty Sainsbury's car park. Going off-road would have been insane. But then along came the Nomad, which looked like a 'normal' Ariel Atom, and was eye-poppingly quick like an Atom but could also mix it on the mud and mucky stuff like a Land Rover.

The Nomad merits a place in this rundown because it can outstrip pretty much any off-roader from zero to triple digits. Plus, the orange exoskeleton frame makes it look like an upside-down Sainsbury's shopping trolley, so it won't look out of place in a car park either.

 Power: *235 bhp*

 0–60 mph: *3.4 seconds*

 Top speed: *125 mph*

 Price: *£30,000*

 Stig Factor:

06 *Aston Martin DB10*

06

Sometimes it's good to simply state the obvious. That's what Chris Evans did when he said the gorgeous DB10 was 'one of the best-looking cars of all time'. The fact that only ten were made, and all were driven by Daniel Craig in scenes from the James Bond film *Spectre*, makes the DB10 even more of a sight to behold. This beauty also has a beast of an engine, using the 4.7-litre V8 from the Vantage to reach speeds close to 200 mph.

The finer details are top secret, of course, but we do have a price — a DB10 sold for nearly £2.5 million at auction to a very rich car fanatic.

 Power: *Top secret*

 0–60 mph: *Top secret*

 Top Speed: *Top secret*

 Price: *£2,434,500*

 Stig Factor: 🏁🏁🏁🏁🏁

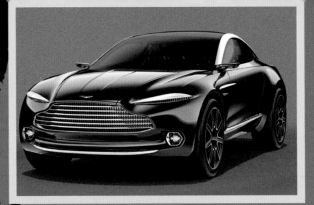

Unlike its chunky all-weather tyres, details about the Aston Martin DBX concept are a bit thin on the ground. All we know for sure is that it will have four-wheel drive, use an electric engine and will appear on the streets of Chelsea and Cheshire around 2020.

Being an Aston, we can probably also assume that it will have a big dollop of power and a fair smattering of speed. Nissan Pathfinders will be left quaking in their Michelins at the traffic lights.

 Power: *Not sure*

 0–60 mph: *5–10 seconds, maybe?*

 Top Speed: *150 mph+ (we hope)*

 Price: *Yes, it will cost some money*

 Stig Factor: 😎😎

07

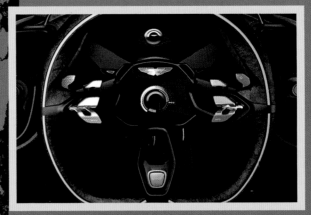

07 *Aston Martin DBX*

Aston Martin One-77

08

You're more likely to catch a glimpse of the Stig morris dancing down Winchester high street than to ever catch a glimpse of an Aston Martin One-77 on the road. Quite appropriately, only 77 of these high-tech hypercars were ever made, which makes them a sight that's rarer than a Simon Cowell smile.

Plus, with an unimaginable 7.3-litre lump of V12 metal under the bonnet, if you do see one you'll probably blink and miss it. So raise the picture on this page up to your nose and take a good, long, hard look at it — it's the closest your eyes will ever get to this ultimate Aston.

Power: 750 bhp

0–60 mph: 3.7 seconds

Top Speed: 220 mph

Price: £1.2 million

Stig Factor:

ASTON MARTIN ONE-77

09 *Aston Martin*
V12 Vantage

The Vantage is still called the 'baby' Aston Martin. Like babies, the Vantage was cute when it was born back in 2005.

But, crucially, it still looks cute eleven years on — unlike an eleven-year-old human that's made of hair gel, Haribo and hormones. Plus we don't know of any toddlers who can scarper across the ground at 200 mph or scuttle from a standstill to 100 mph in 8.4 seconds. So think of the top-of-the-range V12 Vantage S as being more like the rich kid at school who was clever, cool, sporty, well-liked and happy to take long trips through Europe every summer.

 Power: 565 bhp

 0–60 mph: 3.7 seconds

 Top Speed: 205 mph

 Price: £138,000

 Stig Factor:

Vulcan was the ancient Roman god of fire and volcanoes. The Aston Martin Vulcan spits flames from its titanium side-exhaust system. As names go, it's a perfect marriage of mythology and motoring madness.

This track-focused demon is utterly ridiculous but utterly amazing — from its supersized spoiler to the fearsome front splitter and right back to its deadly diffuser. It's up there with the Ferrari FXX K and the McLaren P1 GTR as the most fun you'll have in a racing harness. A speed machine, pure and simple, but one that can crack 200 mph while barbecuing sausages on its side skirts.

 Power: *820 bhp*

 0–60 mph: *3 seconds*

 Top Speed: *200 mph+*

 Price: *£1.8 million*

 Stig Factor:

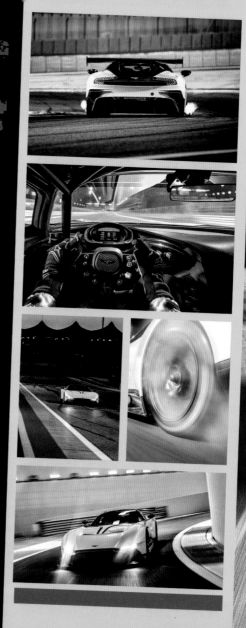

10

Aston Martin
Vulcan

11 Audi R8 V10

Much like 'tasty' and 'sprouts', we're not sure if the words 'everyday' and 'supercar' should be used in the same sentence.

But if you had to pick a car to drive seven days a week that also happened to be knee-tremblingly quick, then the Audi R8 V10 would be it. The Germans don't make their first-ever supercar with a V8 engine any longer, which means owners must manage with a 5.2-litre V10 that conjures up 533 bhp and will get you to 100 mph in about seven seconds. If that's not enough, there's an R8 Plus model that delivers 602 bhp. And remember that the boot is in the front on the R8, in case you stop to pick up some sprouts from the greengrocer.

Power: 533 bhp

0–60 mph: 3.5 seconds

Top Speed: 199 mph

Price: £119,500

Stig Factor:

11

12 *Audi RS 3*

12

The universal definition of a hot hatch is a small, fast four-seater that you can easily chuck a chest of drawers in the back of. The Audi RS3 ticks all those boxes, but it's so hot you might have to pack a fire extinguisher to stop your furniture from going up in flames.

Top Gear loves everything about this Audi — the four-wheel drive, the seven-speed dual-clutch gearbox, the 2.5-litre, five-pot turbo engine . . . We could go on, but someone has just asked us to transport a bedside cabinet from London to Leeds, pronto. Should be fun!

 Power: 362 bhp

 0–60 mph: 4.3 seconds

 Top Speed: 174 mph

 Price: £39,295

 Stig Factor:

If the RS 3 whisks small furniture from A to B at impressive speeds, the RS 6 Avant can take a wardrobe from A to Z even quicker! Quite frankly, this is too much of a good thing – who really needs supercar performance from an all-wheel-drive estate?

But if that is your thang, you'll be over the moon with the performance model's near-600 bhp and 4.0-litre V8 loveliness.

Just warn your neighbours every time you reverse off the driveway, otherwise they could think a jumbo jet is about to land on their house. In other words, it's a bit loud.

 Power: 597 bhp

 0–60 mph: 3.7 seconds

 Top Speed: 189 mph

 Price: £86,000

 Stig Factor:

Viewed from the front, this baby Audi might look a little normal and a bit 'blah'. But move round to the back and you'll see **FOUR EXHAUSTS**. We reckon that any car that has four shiny silver pipes poking out from its behind must automatically be a tad quick and a tad special.

Sticking with that number, the S1 also has four-wheel drive, a four-cylinder 2.0-litre turbocharged engine, four seats and four doors in the Sportback flavour. The only thing that stops it getting a Stig Factor rating of four helmets is that you need to be four-foot-four tall to enjoy sitting in the cramped rear seats.

 Power: 231 bhp

 0–60 mph: 5.8 seconds

 Top Speed: 155 mph

 Price: £24,905

 Stig Factor:

14

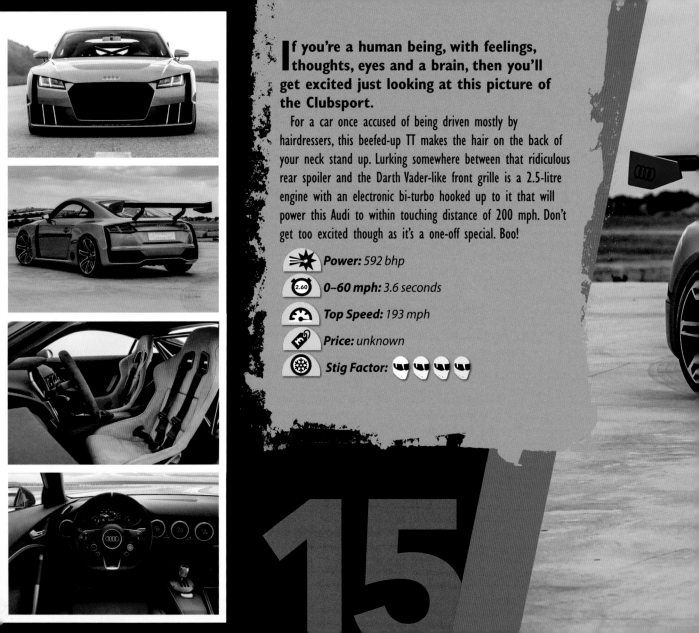

If you're a human being, with feelings, thoughts, eyes and a brain, then you'll get excited just looking at this picture of the Clubsport.

For a car once accused of being driven mostly by hairdressers, this beefed-up TT makes the hair on the back of your neck stand up. Lurking somewhere between that ridiculous rear spoiler and the Darth Vader-like front grille is a 2.5-litre engine with an electronic bi-turbo hooked up to it that will power this Audi to within touching distance of 200 mph. Don't get too excited though as it's a one-off special. Boo!

Power: 592 bhp

0–60 mph: 3.6 seconds

Top Speed: 193 mph

Price: unknown

Stig Factor: 🏎🏎🏎🏎

15

15 Audi TT Clubsport

16 *Avtoros Shaman*

You may well wonder how something that tops out at 50 mph makes a list of 100 fastest cars. Sure, your grandad's lawnmower could outrun it from the lights, but can your grandad's lawnmower do that speed across swamps, hills, forests and even 20-foot-deep rivers?

We thought not. We're also sure you've spotted this Russian-built beast has eight 1.2-metre-tall wheels, with the front and rear four steering independently for better agility. The Shaman is definitely going to have the guys down at Kwik Fit scratching their heads.

 Power: 176 bhp

 0–60 mph: n/a (see below)

 Top Speed: 50 mph

 Price: £88,000

 Stig Factor:

11 **BAC** *Mono*

When a few British car enthusiasts get together, start a company, buy a garage on an industrial estate and design a car, strange things can happen. Take the Mono for example.

It was created by a handful of clever chaps in Liverpool and will match a £1 million Bugatti Veyron on a march from zero to 60. It manages this by weighing about as much as a packet of crisps and having a bespoke 2.5-litre engine that cranks out 526 bhp per tonne. Having room to carry just one person also helps it bother big boys like a LaFerrari or a McLaren P1.

 Power: *305 bhp*

 0–60 mph: *2.8 seconds*

 Top Speed: *170 mph*

 Price: *£124,225*

 Stig Factor:

18 Bentley Bentayga

Silly name, silly price, silly looks and very, very, very silly speeds. That sums up the Bentayga perfectly. Done. Except we need to write a few more words to fill this page out. Er . . . let's go back to the speed bit then. Looking at the numbers listed below, you can quite clearly see it's the fastest SUV on the planet.

Even lightly touching the accelerator with a ballet shoe will transport this 2.2-tonne 4x4 into another galaxy. Not that you'd notice, given that it's as comfortable and luxurious as Buckingham Palace inside. Silly. Just totally silly.

 Power: 600 bhp

 0–60 mph: 4 seconds

 Top Speed: 187 mph

 Price: £160,000

 Stig Factor:

19   Bentley
Continental GT3-R

Back in 2003, no one knew what an iPhone, a Boris bike or a Justin Bieber was. They did know what a Bentley Continental was, because that year the first one rolled off the production line in Crewe. Fast forward to the present and the big British supercar is still going strong – quicker, cooler and more expensive than ever.

Top of the class in all those categories is the GT3-R. It's a sort of road-going version of the successful Conti GT3 endurance racer, using a 4.0-litre twin-turbo V8 to propel all of its 2,195 kilograms to a restricted 170 mph. Bit quicker than a Boris bike, then.

 Power: 572 bhp

 0–60 mph: 3.6 seconds

 Top Speed: 170 mph

 Price: £237,500

 Stig Factor:

We've spent so long on the phone to Bentley, asking if they will actually build this two-seater concept sports car, that our mobile bill will probably cost the same as a production Speed 6 would. To our eyes this Bentley looks more like a chunkier Aston Martin Vantage than a slimmed-down Continental.

And going by looks and name alone, a real-life Speed 6 would have to be a speed machine. Rumour has it that its 4.0-litre bi-turbo V8 engine would have battery-powered electric motors. If it still hasn't gone into production by the time you're reading this, get on the phone to Bentley and ask them why not.

 Power: Unknown

 0–60 mph: Unknown

 Top Speed: Unknown

 Price: Unknown

 Stig Factor:

Bentley EXP 10 Speed 6

21 BMW
3.0 CSL Hommage R

Some things in the 1970s were rubbish, like haircuts, TV shows and football kits. But some things were great, like the BMW 3.0 CSL. A monstrous mix of aluminium alloy, Perspex windows and a Big Ben-sized bumper that was built to race – and win – on American circuits.

The Hommage R is a modern version of that classic and is the best-looking BMW concept ever. Note the word 'concept', as BMW say this rocket racer will never go into production. Which also reminds us of car-factory strikes back in the 70s. Ask your grandad.

Power: *Unknown*

0–60mph: *Unknown*

Top Speed: *Unknown*

Price: *Unknown*

Stig Factor: 🏎🏎🏎🏎

BMW i8

BMW i8 Concept

Part supercar, part eco car, part spaceship – when the i8 landed in 2014 it caused quite a stir.

The brainy BMW bods took a 1.5-litre, three-cylinder turbo engine from a MINI and hooked it up to an electric motor to knock out performance numbers to rival those of V8 fossil-fuel fiends. So you can go very fast and be very happy that trees and polar bears the world over are not suffering because of it. Probably. You'll also be cooler than a polar bear in this car.

 Power: *362 bhp*

 0–60mph: *4.4 seconds*

 Top Speed: *155 mph*

 Price: *£104,485*

 Stig Factor:

When BMW plonked the 2 series in its shiny showrooms, no one really paid any attention until a couple of years later when they stuck the fatter and faster M2 next to it.

From the bespoke tyres to the bulging wheel arches and fearsome exhausts, this shouty little thing holds its head high alongside bigger brothers the M3, M4 and M5. A mini menace good for 155 mph — or 168 mph if your coin can cover the M Driver's Package — the M2 is also, with all that power, good for a spot of sideways driving. But don't try that until the showroom salesman isn't looking . . .

 Power: 370 bhp

 0–60 mph: 4.5 seconds

 Top Speed: 155 mph

 Price: £44,070

 Stig Factor:

23

BMW M2

The M4 motorway is a 192-mile stretch of boring road that runs from west London to Wales.

The BMW M4 is an exciting German coupé that runs from zero to 60 mph in four seconds. Apart from the name, however, the two clearly share no other motoring DNA. The Beemer's absurd 444 bhp arrives thanks to a 3.0-litre V6 engine strapped to a pair of titanic turbos. Quite sensibly the top speed is limited to 155 mph, but unrestricted it will hit 170 mph. The fastest you're permitted to go on the M4 road is 70 mph — we told you the two had zilch in common.

 Power: 444 bhp

 0–60mph: 4.1 seconds

 Top Speed: 155 mph

 Price: £57,050

 Stig Factor:

Sadly, it's time to mourn the fact that the Bugatti Veyron is no longer the world's fastest production car. Sob.

But, the world's newest fastest production car is still a big, bulking, beastly Bugatti — just one that goes by the name of Chiron. Yay! You'll probably read the numbers below and think a baby has been typing randomly on our keyboard. However, these figures are correct. The Chiron's 8.0-litre quad-turbo W16 engine delivers 1,479 bhp for a restricted top speed of 261 mph. Another frightening number is that you'll need £1.9 million to own one. Sob, sob.

 Power: *1,479 bhp*

 0–60 mph: *2.5 seconds*

 Top Speed: *261 mph*

 Price: *£1.9 million*

 Stig Factor:

Bugatti
Veyron GSV

GSV stands for 'Grand Sport Vitesse'. It could also mean 'Gotta Speedy Vehicle' if you're a bit of a show-off.

Which, quite honestly, you would have to be to have paid out for one of the most hyped hypercars in the galaxy. The Veyron flies straight into any countdown of quickest cars, but the GSV also sets a very unusual speed record: world's fastest umbrella. You see, this model is a convertible and comes with a carbon-fibre umbrella to snap into the roofline should the heavens open. That's both clever and crazy — two words *Top Gear* likes.

  Power: 1,200 bhp

 0–60mph: 2.5 seconds

 Top Speed: 260 mph

 Price: £2 million

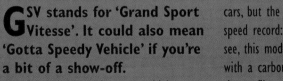   **Stig Factor:**

27 Caparo T1

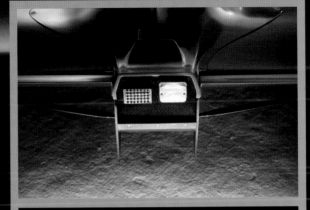

About 20 billion Ford Focus cars have been sold around the world. We reckon only about 20 Caparos have. That means there are 19,980,000,000 glum owners behind the wheels of Fords and 20 stupidly happy owners inside their T1s.

The Caparo claims to be the closest a road-going car can get to being a Formula One machine. It certainly has the speed, acceleration, agility and looks of an F1 racer, but also lights and indicators that make it possible to drive on public roads. You'll get about 6 billion envious looks from the public if you do.

 Power: *575 bhp*

 0–60mph: *2.5 seconds*

 Top Speed: *200 mph*

 Price: *£190,000*

 Stig Factor:

27

You know if you need to wear a crash helmet to drive a car it's going to be very tasty and very quick. Actually, you don't have to wear a lid behind the wheel of a 620R, but if you do it means you won't swallow 756 flies every time you go out in it. Which would not be very tasty.

With 580 bhp per tonne and a power-to-weight ratio that outmuscles Veyrons and McLaren F1s, the Caterham can live with any supercar on a short, straight road. It's pretty tasty on the corners too.

 Power: 311 bhp

 0–60mph: 2.8 seconds

Top Speed: 155 mph

Price: £49,995

Stig Factor:

GN13 GZA

Traditionally, American dudes called Hank, Chip and Chad like to buy Chevy Corvettes.

Since the new and improved 6.2-litre Z06 arrived, British chaps called Colin, Graham and Nigel could be buying them too. With those looks, and that long, sweeping bonnet, it's still undeniably a 'Vette. But there's now a touch of Ferrari in its appearance as well, and definitely Ferrari-levels of power under that bonnet.

A comfortable, road-going motor that can tickle 200 mph for less than £70K? Accountants called Colin, Graham and Nigel will like the sound of that.

 Power: *650 bhp*

 0–60mph: *3.8 seconds*

 Top Speed: *199 mph*

 Price: *£67,331*

 Stig Factor:

29

29 *Chevrolet* Corvette Z06

30

30 *Cadillac* CTS-V

In the early 1980s Cadillacs used to have so many straight lines, sharp bits and 90-degree corners that you risked severing a limb every time you walked past one.

And, given that they were the size of an aircraft carrier, they took a long time to walk past. Mercifully, in the mid-2010s they are a bit curvier, a bit leaner, a bit shorter and a bit faster.

Quite a bit faster in fact, with the CTS-V licking it all the way to 200 mph to take the crown of fastest-ever production Caddy. God bless America, we say.

 Power: *640 bhp*

 0–60mph: *3.8 seconds*

 Top Speed: *200 mph*

 Price: *£98,000*

    Stig Factor:

Three things make any car faster: big racing stripes, a humongous spoiler and a Stig.

Since the Viper ACR already has two of these (and the third can be arranged if Dodge ever find the Stig's mobile phone number*), it's a sure bet to be lightning quick. Except that ridiculous 1.8-metre wide rear wing doesn't make the Viper faster — it's part of the Extreme Aero Package, which reduces top speed from 200 mph to 177 mph, but boosts the handling big time. It looks cool, so that's fine by us.

 Power: 645 bhp

 0–60mph: 3.5 seconds

 Top Speed: 177 mph

 Price: £85,000 approx

 Stig Factor:

*The Stig doesn't have a mobile phone.

MICHIGAN
032 M 997

When Ferrari sat down to design a car that would be better than the 458, this was their wish list: more power, more speed and looks good in red.

What they came up with was the 488 GTB. It has 100 more bhp than the 458 (tick). It goes 6 mph faster (tick). It looks stunning in red (tick). In all honesty, this 488 is so good and so fast

that even if it was covered in pink and brown spots with purple stars Premier League footballers would still snap it up.

 Power: 661 bhp

 0–60mph: 3 seconds

 Top Speed: 205 mph

 Price: £183,974

 Stig Factor:

32 *Ferrari 488 GTB*

33 Ferrari F12tdf

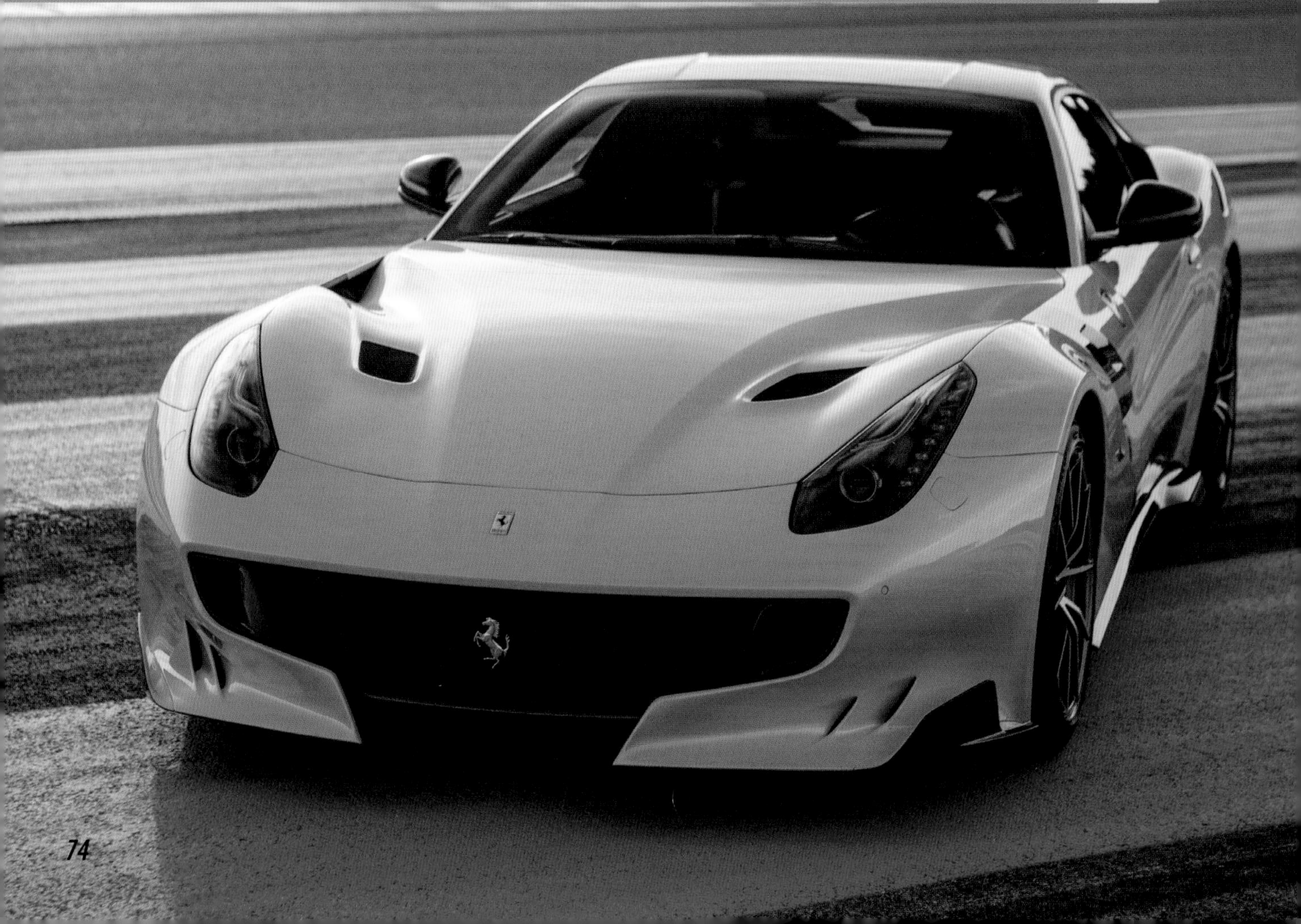

Top Gear **is not convinced there are aliens searching for Planet Earth.**

But, if a three-eyed green monster landed its spaceship right next to the Ferrari F12tdf, it would take one look and fly straight off again. That's because this 6.3-litre V12 monster just doesn't look like something the human race could possibly conceive, let alone actually create and crank around on public roads alongside Kia Cee'ds and Vauxhall Astras. The F12tdf's speed and power is utterly out of this world — even three-eyed green monsters know that.

 Power: *770 bhp*

 0–60mph: *2.9 seconds*

 Top Speed: *211 mph*

Price: *£339,000*

Stig Factor: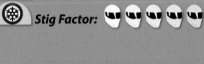

33

LaFerrari blows all other Ferraris off the road, the track, Earth, the solar system, the galaxy, the universe ... we'll have to leave it there as we never paid enough attention in our planetary physics lessons.

Putting aside its weird name — the human equivalent of being called Jeff TheJeff — everything about Ferrari's ultimate road car is totally, totally mind-blowing. The power, the top speed, the acceleration, the torque, those wing mirrors. To us it's as mesmerising as the bell at the end of the school day. Arrgghh! Enough with the school references!

 Power: 950 bhp

 0–60mph: sub-3 seconds

 Top Speed: 217 mph+

 Price: £1.15 million

 Stig Factor:

34

Mazda sells shed-loads of little MX-5 convertibles.

Fiat doesn't sell many these days, so the Italians decided to give Japan a call and work together on a lovely new drop-top. Which is to say, basically copy all the good bits from the MX-5 and glue on a few Fiat badges.

As it happens, the idea worked quite well, and when the 124 Spider was unveiled in 2016 it looked and drove much like a menacing Mazda should. Now Fiat just needs to sell quite a lot of the turbocharged 1.4-litre toys to make that phone call worthwhile.

 Power: 138 bhp

 0–60mph: 8 seconds approx

 Top Speed: 120 mph

 Price: £20,000

 Stig Factor:

35

35 Fiat 124 Spider

36 Ford Fiesta ST200

Owning a motor that your Auntie Ruth also has is nothing to brag about.

An exception would be if Auntie Ruth has a Fiesta 1.0-litre EcoBoost while you have a Fiesta ST200. One has 99 bhp, the other has 197 bhp. One will rocket to 140 mph, whereas the other might make 90 mph by next Tuesday. Owning a Fiesta ST200 really is something to boast about, not least because only 500 are made each year, but also because of its hair-raising hot-hatch speed, its superb handling and its sporty looks. Hopefully Auntie Ruth won't upgrade to one too and ruin your street cred.

 Power: 197 bhp

 0–60mph: 6.7 seconds

 Top Speed: 140 mph

 Price: £21,000 approx

Stig Factor: 👿👿👿👿

There's a magic button inside the frighteningly fast Ford Focus RS. It's beside the gearstick and is labelled 'drive mode'.

Press that and you can pick four different ways to set up your RS. Normal mode is, well, for normal driving. Sport mode is a bit fruitier, and likewise the Track setting. The fourth and final mode is Drift — that's the one that should come with a government health-and-safety warning. It gives the car and the owner the potential to drive sideways and make lots of smoke from the wheels. We suggest you don't drive like that unless you happen to be called the Stig. Which you don't.

 Power: 345 bhp

 0–60mph: 4.7 seconds

 Top Speed: 165 mph

 Price: £29,995

Stig Factor:

Ford *Focus RS*

38 Ford GT

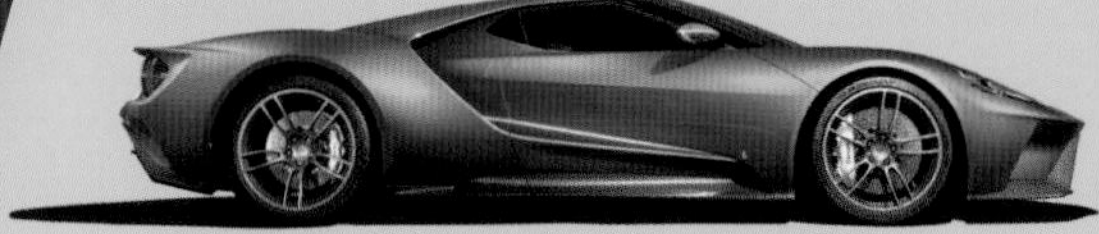

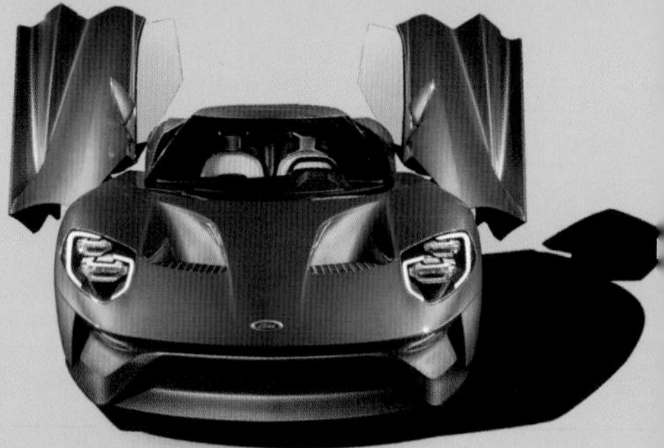

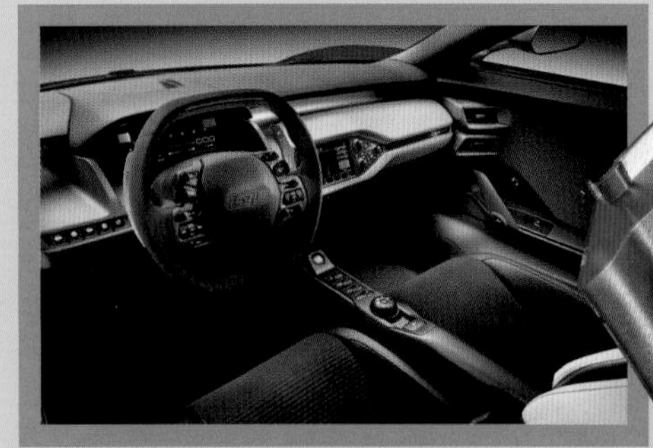

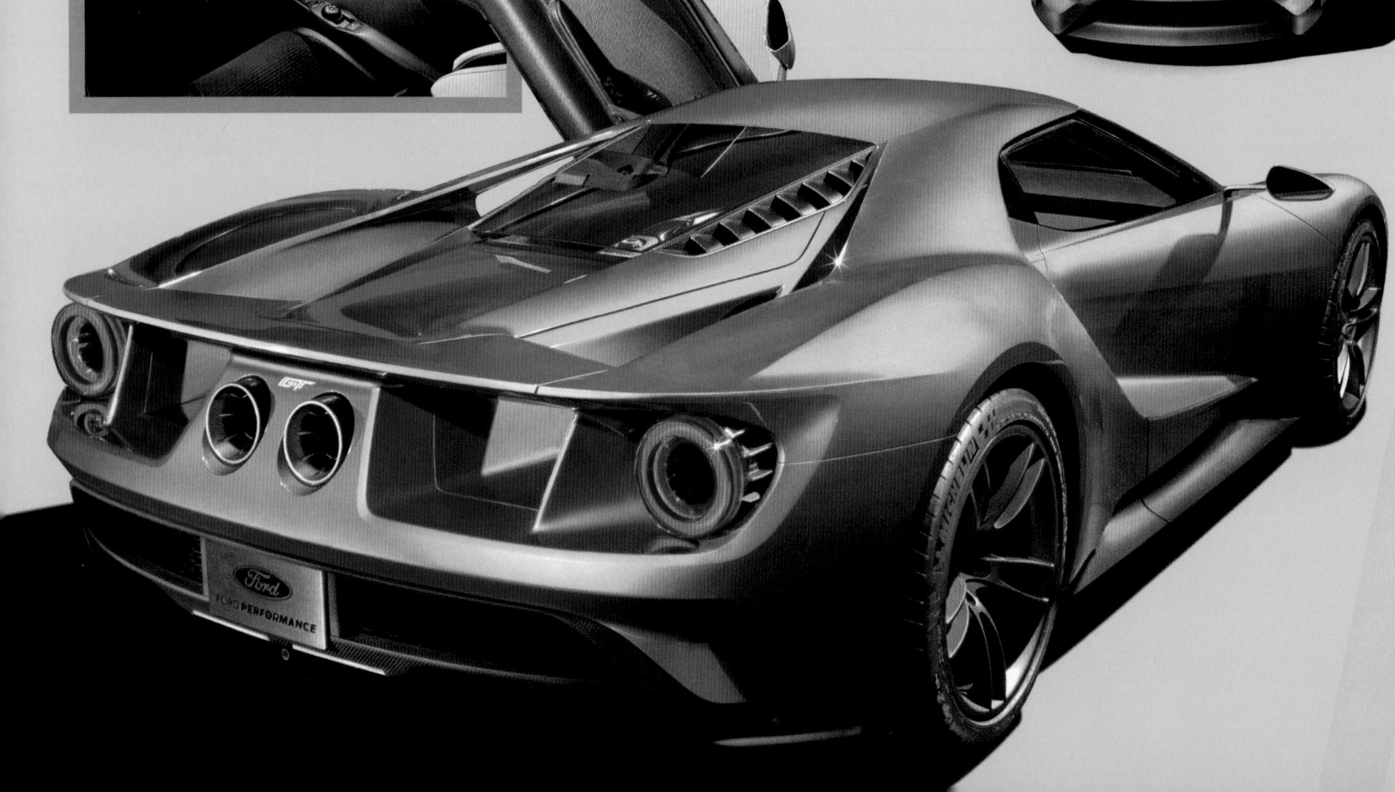

38

The Ford GT40 was created in 1964 specifically to annoy Ferrari, which it did by blitzing the Italians in the 24 Hours of Le Mans race four years in a row.

It then made a comeback in 2004, but only annoyed its select few owners who'd paid £125,000 for a car that was a bit unreliable. And then in 2016 it was reborn for a third time — with more power, more speed,

better looks, increased aero and an alarm that doesn't go off every fourteen minutes. It went on to win its class in Le Mans in 2016.

 Power: *600 bhp +*

 0–60mph: *3.3 seconds*

 Top Speed: *200 mph*

 Price: *£200,00–250,000*

 Stig Factor:

39 Hennessey *Venom GT*

omewhere underneath the Hennessey Venom GT a Lotus Exige. ook for it behind the strapping 7.0-litre twin-turbo engine, or maybe to the right the carbon-ceramic brakes, or just inside adjustable rear wing. It's in there. *Top* ar likes the fact that awesome American

sports-car creator Hennessey dumped all its expensive, hi-tech bits and pieces on a lovely little Lotus from Norfolk to concoct what Hennessey says is the fastest production car ever. There's some debate as to whether it can actually claim that crown, but there's no debating a Lotus lies within.

 Power: *1,244 bhp*

 0–60mph: *2.4 seconds*

 Top Speed: *270 mph*

 Price: *£800,000*

 Stig Factor:

39

40 *Honda Civic Type R*

40

If Honda gave *Top Gear* a Type R to drive for a year, that wouldn't be a bad thing.

The only problem is we don't think we'd get very far, because every morning we'd stand and look at it for ages and forget to drive it. Then night would fall, our eyes would droop and we'd have to go to bed. The same process would be repeated the next day and the day after that. This is because *Top Gear* can't decide if it likes the look of the Type R or not. We've been told it's a pocket rocket to drive, but whether we'd actually experience that ourselves is debatable.

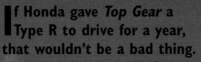

 Power: *306 bhp*

 0–60mph: *5.7 seconds*

 Top Speed: *167 mph*

 Price: *£32,995*

 Stig Factor:

To buy an original NSX you needed to be a bit rich and a bit bonkers.

You also needed to be a bit rich and a bit bonkers between 1990 and 2005, when Honda knocked them out to any old yob. Then, about seven years after they'd stopped building this brute, Honda said they were creating a new NSX. So the rich and bonkers people waited for it . . . then they waited some more. Eventually, more than four years after Honda had said the new supercar was coming, it finally arrived. With 573 bhp from a 3.5-litre V6 and three clever electric motors, it's certainly speedy. It just hasn't been speedy getting to the showroom.

 Power: *573 bhp*

 0–60mph: *3.2 seconds*

 Top Speed: *190 mph*

 Price: *£130,000 approx*

 Stig Factor:

Supply and demand – that's what the car industry is all about.

So, presumably, a sheep farmer in Australia once demanded a utility van to transport a few of his animals in the back of very, very quickly. Holden Super Vehicles, being the crazy Australian performance-car manufacturers that they are, duly supplied such a vehicle. It's called the Maloo and is a 6.2-litre supercharged V8 that's more back to the future than outback, but at least the Ozzie sheep farmer's problem was solved. Job done.

 Power: 573 bhp

 0–60mph: 3.2 seconds

 Top Speed: 190 mph

 Price: £60,000 approx

 Stig Factor:

43 *Infiniti Q50*
Eau Rouge

Top *Gear* liked the Infiniti Q50, with its thumping 400-bhp, 3.0-litre twin-turbo V6.

But then *Top Gear* drove the Eau Rouge version, which dished out 560 bhp from its Nissan GT-R engine and racked up 60 mph in just four seconds. So Top Gear told Infiniti to stick the weedy 400-bhp model where the sun doesn't shine ... then Infiniti spoiled the party by saying they wouldn't make the hardcore Eau Rouge super saloon after all — it would remain just a concept.

Top Gear felt a bit silly, and we pretended that we'd preferred the 400-bhp version more anyway. Infiniti didn't believe us and politely told *Top Gear* to go away.

Power: *560 bhp*

0–60mph: *4 seconds*

Top Speed: *160 mph approx*

Price: *Unknown*

Stig Factor: 🏁🏁🏁

43

Concept supercars are both good things and bad things. They're good when a cool car designer sits down and sketches one.

They're even better when a car manufacturer takes that sketch and starts to build it. But they're bad when we see this dream machine on a track, only to be told that it will never actually make production. That's like your mum telling you that you can eat your own bodyweight in ice cream, only to then say all the ice cream in the world has disappeared forever.

So think of the hybrid-powered C-X75 as the world's quickest ice cream that you'll never get to lick. Or something like that.

 Power: 900 bhp

 0–60mph: 3 seconds

 Top Speed: 184 mph

 Price: Unknown

 Stig Factor:

44 Jaguar C-X75

Jaguars used to be owned by people called Nigel. Some, like the S-TYPE of the 90s, were as big as an electricity pylon and about as good-looking.

Safe to say, then, that Jags haven't always had a great image. But then the XK came along and all that started to change. When the F-TYPE arrived, Jags were safely back in the realm of cool cars to be driven by cool people. One of the coolest and quickest is the F-TYPE SVR, which has a heavenly 5.0-litre V8 and power to match a Ferrari 458. Keep away from this one please, Nigel.

 Power: *567 bhp*

 0–60mph: *3.8 seconds*

Top Speed: *200 mph*

Price: *£110,000*

Stig Factor:

45

For years, the most famous cars to come out of Sweden were boring Volvos. Then, at the start of the twenty-first century, Swedish supercars appeared from a company called Koenigsegg.

Not only was this a difficult car to spell and say, but it was also a difficult car to spot. Only a handful were made each year, and on the road they shot past your eyes before your brain could process the image. First the CCX model

and then the Agera finally gave Swedes a proper car that they could properly shout about, which left boring Volvo estates to contemplate a life lugging boring furniture from boring IKEA.

 Power: *1,115 bhp*

 0–60mph: *2.8 seconds*

Top Speed: *273 mph*

Price: *£875,000*

Stig Factor:

46 *Koenigsegg Agera*

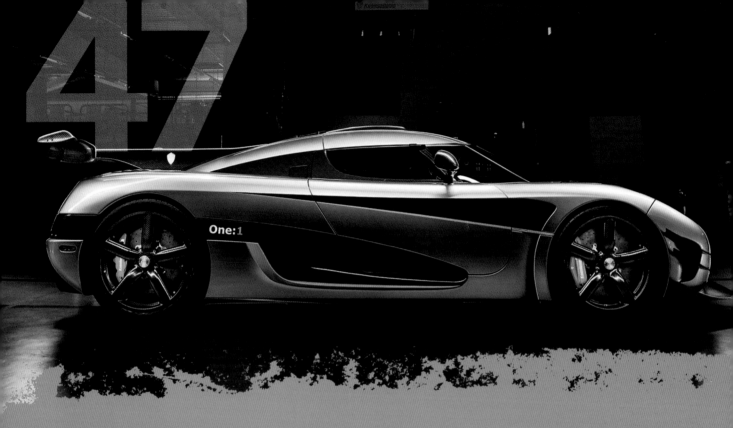

47

Koenigsegg do not call the One:1 a supercar. They don't even label it a hypercar.

The Swedish company says it's a 'megacar', so-called because it's the world's first production car to produce a megawatt of power. It's mega amazing, that's for sure, with crazy acceleration, a brutal top speed and a price tag to cause even a Saudi prince to scratch his chin. Only six were made for sale, and *Top Gear* would love to get our hands on just one of those One:1s one day.

 Power: 1,322 bhp

 0–60mph: 2.8 seconds

 Top Speed: 273 mph

 Price: £1.7 million

 Stig Factor:

Going 135 mph when your bottom is about 3 mm off the ground is really rather frightening. And, as the X-BOW will want to do that speed on the straight roads and the bendy bits, it becomes even more of a hair-raising experience.

It shouldn't come as a total surprise, though, because KTM are famous for making mega-quick motorbikes for people who probably enjoy the taste of tarmac. *Top Gear* is not one of those people, and neither do we enjoy the taste of flies — don't forget your helmet if you venture out in this crazy car-bike-cart combo.

 Power: 240 bhp

 0–60mph: 3.9 seconds

 Top Speed: 135 mph

 Price: £62,000+

 Stig Factor:

A bog-standard Lamborghini Aventador LP 750-4 is a supercar that's already rammed with more power than the Large Hadron Collider.

But the loons at Lambo weren't happy with that, so they stripped out some weight, stuck a new exhaust on, and tweaked the gearbox and a few other things to end up with the Superveloce. The result was sub-three seconds from zero to 60 mph and just 24 seconds to reach 186 mph. In the money stakes,

the SV is also a bit of a bargain because it keeps up with hypercars three times its price. We hope you're happy with it now, Mr Lamborghini, because everyone else is.

 Power: *750 bhp*

 0–60mph: *2.9 seconds*

 Top Speed: *217 mph*

 Price: *£315,000*

 Stig Factor:

49 Lamborghini
Aventador LP 750-4 SV

EW 936PA

49

50

50 *Lamborghini* Egoista

When Lamborghini celebrated their fiftieth birthday, they gave themselves a present.

It was called the Egoista and looked like a cross between an attack plane, a UFO and a Transformer — with a touch of Batmobile thrown in just for good measure. It's main selling point (not that you could buy it, as only one was built and Lambo, quite rightly, kept it for themselves) was that it had anti-radar carbon-fibre bodywork so the 'enemy' couldn't detect it. It's a car that cracks 200 mph, has orange wheels and has flashing LEDs on its roof. That makes it very detectable in our book.

Power: *Unknown*

0–60mph: *4 seconds*

Top Speed: *200 mph*

Price: *Priceless*

Stig Factor:

Lamborghini don't do understatement. Everything they do is big, bold, bright and baffling.

Even though the Huracán, the baby of its supercar bunch, has no scissor doors or spoilers like the Adventador it still has all the looks and power that a Lambo should. There's even a flip-open ignition switch, which makes you feel like you're in a fighter jet every time you start the engine. You will feel like a pilot too, given the speed available under your right foot. Whether you're six or 76, the Huracán puts a massive smile across your chops — and that's no understatement.

 Power: *602 bhp*

 0–60mph: *3.2 seconds*

Top Speed: *202 mph*

Price: *£187,000*

Stig Factor:

51

51 *Lamborghini*
Huracán LP610-4

When Lamborghini first showed *Top Gear* the Centenario – a car which celebrates the one-hundreth birthday of founder, Ferruccio Lamborghini – we asked how fast it was in reverse.

This was because all 40 of the lucky owners will drive it backwards all the time, just to show off that rear diffuser. Take a look at the back of it — it's like a giant carbon-fibre cheese grater crossed with a Dalek. Lamborghini didn't tell us how fast reverse gear is, and reminded us that in a more accustomed forward motion the Centenario hits nearly 220 mph, but we weren't listening because we couldn't stop looking at that rear diffuser.

 Power: *760 bhp+*

 0–60mph: *2.8 seconds*

 Top Speed: *217 mph+*

 Price: *£1.7 million*

 Stig Factor:

Like a terrier chasing its tail, Lamborghini went a bit crazy in the twenty-first century. They were forever outdoing their own freakily fast limited-edition hypercars.

First came the Reventon, then the Sesto Elemento, followed by the Veneno. Each one more ridiculous, more ferocious and more exclusive than its predecessor, with the Veneno's awesome carbon-fibre fin and rear spoiler doing something special to help push it past 220 mph. It's louder than a volcano, thunder and Godzilla combined, and a cracker to look at. Keep chasing your tail please, Lamborghini.

 Power: *740 bhp*

 0–60mph: *2.9 seconds*

 Top Speed: *221 mph*

 Price: *£2.8 million*

 Stig Factor:

53 *Lamborghini* Veneno

We know the 2.2-litre Defender 110 doesn't pull up any trees on the motorway. But stick it on a farm, a field or a filthy hill and it will pull up plenty of trees, horseboxes and trailers at a more-than-appropriate speed.

It's an iconic and complete off-roader, and as much a part of the British landscape as church towers, thatched cottages and McDonald's drive-throughs. Over 2 million

Defenders were made in the 67 years it was built and driven by everyone from the Queen to James Bond. *Top Gear* will defend its right to be in this book all day long.

 Power: 122 bhp

 0–60mph: 14.7 seconds

 Top Speed: 90 mph

 Price: No longer sold

 **Stig Factor:**

Everyone chuckled when Lexus announced they were building a supercar.

The luxury Japanese manufacturer had a reputation for making saloon and hybrid SUVs that were as unexciting as a National Trust house on a wet bank holiday. However, when they presented the LFA, everyone stopped laughing and started applauding. Their 4.8-litre V10 creation could take on a DBS, Gallardo and a Ferrari 599 without breaking a sweat and was like a high-tech spaceship inside. The only thing people didn't applaud was the price of all this speed and sophistication: six times more than a Nissan GT-R. Ouch.

 Power: 552 bhp

 0–60mph: 3.7 seconds

 Top Speed: 202 mph

 Price: £340,000

 Stig Factor:

55

Top Gear loves an underdog. When the 5.0-litre V8 Lexus RC F squared up to the BMW M4, Audi RS5 and Merc C63 AMG for a sports coupé face-off, we stood firmly in its corner.

It didn't win and we never expected it to — in truth the Lexus never really came close to knocking out the Germans. But we admired its pluckiness and sheer blind faith in causing an upset. At £60,000, the RC F is a sixth of the price of the range-topping LFA but packs all the speed and power you'll ever need. Plus, there's room to pack a couple of pet dogs on the rear seats.

 Power: 471 bhp

 0–60mph: 4.5 seconds

 Top Speed: 168 mph

 Price: £60,000

Stig Factor: 🎭🎭🎭

Why did Lotus name their new hardcore sports car the 3-Eleven?

Thankfully, it does have more than 311 bhp, it's much less than £311,000 and, unlike the Lotus Elise, it won't break down every 311 metres. This mean machine's moniker derives from the fact there are just 311 models in existence, making it very exclusive as well as very fast. Driving this supercharged 3.5-litre V6 almost every day would be a total blast, with every other Sunday and bank holiday to wash it and admire it on your driveway. Which equates to about 311 days of total driving pleasure every year.

 Power: 410 bhp

 0–60mph: 3.3 seconds

 Top Speed: 180 mph

 Price: £86,000

 Stig Factor: 🏁🏁🏁🏁

AU15 BTV

57

58 *Lotus* Exige 3.5 V6 S

The people of Norfolk see lots of tractors, caravans and holiday-seeking Hyundai i30s on their roads.

But, because Lotus HQ is in the middle of their county, they're also treated to the epic sight of the Exige blasting along country lanes and turning heads on the A1064 between Billockby and Fleggburgh. And, if they're very lucky, that Exige will be the 3.5 V6 S — a supercharged mini menace with a power-to-weight ratio of a 911 Turbo. If the locals need still further proof of how explosive this particular Exige is, it comes with its own fire extinguisher. That's hot news in Hemsby and Horsey.

 Power: 345 bhp

 0–60mph: 3.8 seconds

 Top Speed: 170 mph

 Price: £53,000

 Stig Factor: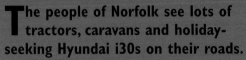

125

Maserati dilly-dallied for years about whether to build the gorgeous Alfieri concept.

However, *Top Gear* lives in a universe where it does exist and where our neighbours all own them. This is good because we get to see and hear it from the comfort of our living room, and occasionally one of our neighbours — let's call him Steve — takes us for a ride in it. This is also good, because we get to experience the power and speed we imagine it would have, without the headache of maintenance and bills that come with any Maserati supercar . . . even an imaginary one owned by Steve.

Power: *560 bhp*

0–60mph: *4 seconds approx*

Top Speed: *180 mph approx*

Price: *Unknown*

Stig Factor:

59

It's not the fastest, the prettiest, the coolest or the cheapest convertible in the world.

It's not even the craziest Mazda ever — that tag belongs to the deceased Furai. But the Mazda MX-5 merits being in this top 100 as much as any supercar. We could say it's the most fun you can have from a 1.5-litre four-cylinder engine, the most fun you can have with less than 130 bhp, and the most fun for under £20,000. Whether you're 25 or 65, the MX-5 will put a grin above your chin. *Top Gear* salutes it.

 Power: *129 bhp*

 0–60mph: *8.8 seconds*

 Top Speed: *125 mph*

 Price: *£19,000*

 Stig Factor:

61 *Mazda RX-Vision*

When Mazda first took the covers off its RX-Vision in 2015, *Top Gear* immediately gave it an award for Best Mazda Production Car on the Planet. Mazda then advised us to take another look at the car's name.

It turns out that 'Vision' means 'concept', and Mazda wasn't sure if this bad boy would ever be seen on the streets of Tokyo, Toronto or, er, Tunbridge Wells. We've taken a punt on what this rotary-engine-powered coupé's speed and acceleration would be and also given it a new award: Best Shiny Red Mazda Concept Car that Looks Fast and Should Definitely Be Built for Real.

 Power: 300 bhp (estimated)

 0–60mph: 5 seconds (estimated)

 Top Speed: 130 mph (estimated)

 Price: £23,000 (estimated)

 Stig Factor:

61

131

McLaren used to be famous for making Formula One cars. Then, in the 1990s and early 2000s, they dabbled in supercars such as the F1 and SLR. A few years on, they dabbled again with the 12C, the 570S and the 650S.

Then in 2015 their continued dabbling led to the appearance of the very fast 675LT — an astonishing car that clocks 124 mph in under eight seconds. LT stands for Long Tail and and in Season 23 of *Top Gear* it set the fastest ever lap for a production car ever!

 Power: *666 bhp*

 0–60mph: *2.9 seconds*

 Top Speed: *205 mph*

 Price: *£259,500*

 Stig Factor:

▼ 62 *McLaren 675LT*

133

63 *McLaren P1*™

Scientists in white coats know that the Earth rotates once round its own axis every 24 hours. That's unless a McLaren P1's engine is running, in which case the entire solar system is sucked through a vortex in six seconds flat and spat out somewhere near what would have been High Wycombe.

You see, the P1 is so powerful and so fast that it has the ability to move planets, time and tides while pretending to be an environmentally friendly thing with an electric motor. It will also rotate its way round the Nürburgring in under seven minutes ... a journey which might need some other chaps in white coats to provide you with medical assistance afterwards.

 Power: 903 bhp

 0–60mph: 2.6 seconds

 Top Speed: 217 mph

 Price: £866,000

 Stig Factor:

Deep within McLaren HQ in Surrey there's a strange room with the words SPECIAL OPERATIONS on the door.

Far from being home to secret spies and soldiers, this is where a few nerdy folk spend all day and night designing and building one-off cars for very rich people. And a few years back those nerdy folk created the X-1 — a terrifying machine that looks like a cross between a 1958 Cadillac and a futuristic flying machine from 2098. Underneath it is a hyped-up McLaren 12C, which boots this beast to over 200 mph. We love it and loathe it all at the same time.

 Power: 617 bhp

 0–60mph: 3.2 seconds (estimat

 Top Speed: 220 mph

 Price: £350,000

 Stig Factor:

64

136

64 *McLaren X-1*

On a hot-hatch scale of one to ten, with one being a bag of frozen peas and ten a vindaloo with extra chillies, the AMG A 45 is firmly in double-digits territory. The power from its 2.0-litre four-cylinder engine is staggering – 60 bhp more than a Golf R, 30 bhp more than a Porsche Boxster GTS – and it takes less than five seconds to reach 60 mph.

In a Top Trumps tussle it blows other sports hatches away, helped also by being one of the most expensive. It's tasty in a straight line and tasty on the corners. Much easier to stomach than that dodgy spicy curry.

Power: 360 bhp

0–60mph: 4.6 seconds

Top Speed: 155 mph

Price: £37,960

Stig Factor:

65

65   *Mercedes-AMG A 45*

66 *Mercedes* S 63 AMG Coupé

Here's a *Top Gear* fact: cars with two doors look better than cars with four doors. And cars with 5.5-litre twin-turbo V8 engines, 577 bhp and four ludicrously loud exhausts look better than just about anything else they cruise past.

This means that no one should buy the four-door saloon S 63 AMG because the coupé kills it in the looks department but can also teleport four full-size adults in full state-visit style. But lots of people are still buying the saloon, which proves another *Top Gear* fact: people don't listen to what *Top Gear* tells them. Or maybe they just didn't hear us over those exhausts.

 Power: *577 bhp*

 0–60mph: *3.9 seconds*

 Top Speed: *155 mph*

 Price: *£124,680*

 Stig Factor:

In 1954 you could buy a cheap and cheerful Ford Anglia. It came with two or four doors, had 40 bhp and cost £500. Or you could buy a Mercedes-Benz 300 SL, which had two gull-wing doors, 210 bhp and cost ten times as much. Fast forward 60-odd years and the equivalent is buying a Ford Fiesta or a Merc SLS Black.

One comes with 622 bhp, a 6.2-litre V8 that kisses 200 mph, and a pair of SL-inspired, jaw-dropping gull-wing doors. The other doesn't. If you have £230,000 stuffed in your piggy bank it's an easy decision. If you don't, *Top Gear* hopes you like your cheap and cheerful Fiesta.*

Power: *622 bhp*

0-60mph: *3.6 seconds*

Top Speed: *196 mph*

Price: *£229,935*

Stig Factor: 🏁🏁🏁🏁

* *Top Gear* knows you won't like your cheap and cheerful Fiesta very much.

67 *Mercedes SLS Black*

The Stig doesn't know what a music and entertainment system is. He doesn't have a clue what an 8.4-inch colour display does, what Bluetooth streaming offers or what a digital radio is. The only in-car entertainment he needs and understands is the entertainment he gets from mashing his right foot to the road and rocketing a sports car from zero to next Sunday in under six seconds.

He'll be eager to get behind the wheel of the 4.0-litre twin-turbo V8 AMG GT S then, because it's more entertaining than Robbie Williams singing 'Let Me Entertain You' while wearing a T-shirt that says I AM MR ENTERTAINMENT on it. Not that the Stig knows who Robbie Williams is.

 Power: 510 bhp

 0–60mph: 3.8 seconds

 Top Speed: 193 mph

 Price: £114,000

 Stig Factor:

69 *Mercedes-Benz*
G 63 AMG 6x6

AMGs are not little run-around cars designed to take you to the garden centre on the weekend and to chess club at the village hall every Wednesday. They are high-tech super saloons, speed-crazy coupés or hilarious hot hatches. Somehow, though, the G-Wagen AMG 6x6 manages to be all of these at once: a comfortable cruiser, a quick sprinter and great fun to drive. Plus, thanks to its six 37-inch wheels, it can be all of these things while driving on the road, sand dunes, Salisbury Plain, Kilimanjaro or Krakatoa. A 6-metre-long superhero supercar, then. Just don't try to park it at the village hall.

Power: *536 bhp*

0–60mph: *6 seconds*

Top Speed: *100 mph*

Price: *£370,000*

Stig Factor:

70

In this book you'll read that Lamborghinis are brilliant because they are big, bold and baffling. But you can still have bags of fun in cars that are compact, cosy and cutesy too – especially if they dish out over 200 bhp and bits of the bodywork are painted red. One such is the MINI John Cooper Works GP.

For a small hot hatch it packs a big old punch and zooms with ease on zigzagging roads and twisty tracks. The Works GP became the fastest ever MINI when it was unleashed in 2013, and even though its roots are more Mr Bean than bold and baffling it's still a cracker in our book.

Power: 215 bhp

0–60mph: 6.3 seconds

Top Speed: 150 mph

Price: £28,790

Stig Factor:

70 **MINI** *John Cooper Works GP*

Take a boring four-door, 2.0-litre saloon and stick a spoiler, a diffuser and an air scoop on it and tweak the engine to NASA-like proportions, and you have the basic recipe for a Mitsubishi Evo X FQ-400. Sort of.

This £50,000 Japanese hooligan shouldn't cause headaches for sophisticated £200,000 Italian supercars. But it does, and to such an extent that Ferrari and Lambo owners are given a free pack of painkillers every time they hand over a cheque. Over the years, Evos have also been made with 305 bhp, 325 bhp and 345 bhp, but it would be a tad boring to drive a ridiculously underpowered saloon like that.

 Power: *403 bhp*

 0–60mph: *3.8 seconds*

 Top Speed: *155 mph*

 Price: *£49,999*

 Stig Factor:

71 *Mitsubishi Evo X FQ-400*

Kids are taught basic rules of the world: Sunday tea at Granny's must be boring, the United Kingdom will never win Eurovision and that cars have four wheels.

So what do six-year-olds think when they first clap eyes on a Morgan 3 Wheeler?

Probably that adults tell great big lies, as clearly some cars have three wheels plus machine guns for exhausts and an engine where the front bumper should be. The Morgan is the fastest thing on three wheels in this book and is a proper production car, even though it looks as unrealistic as your granny's chances of winning Eurovision.

 Power: 115 bhp

 0–60mph: 6 seconds

 Top Speed: 115 mph

 Price: £31,140

 Stig Factor:

The regular Nissan GT-R was never a slouch. With 542 bhp and a zero to 60 mph time of under three seconds, it could get you from Bognor to Birmingham in about 48 seconds – with heavy traffic.

But now the NISMO-tuned GT-R, with 50 bhp more and a bit less weight, can do that journey in about 32 seconds — with heavy traffic. Going via Glasgow. NISMO is like Merc's AMG and BMW's M division — a bunch of clever bods who make quick cars go even quicker. It's all very unnecessary in the real world, but who wants to live in the real world? Not *Top Gear*. And we don't fancy Bognor or Birmingham much either.

 Power: *591 bhp*

 0–60mph: *2.5 seconds*

 Top Speed: *196 mph*

 Price: *£123,855*

 Stig Factor: 🏎🏎🏎🏎

73

73 *Nissan GT-R® NISMO®*

74 Nissan Juke® NISMO®

When *Top Gear* began scribbling names of cars to include in this book, some joker jotted down the Juke. Oh, how the rest of us laughed!

But then that person pointed to a picture of a Juke that NISMO, Nissan's performance-tuning people, had worked over with a few shiny spanners. We all stopped laughing and started staring at the performance figures. With 218 horses under its frog-like bonnet and speeds to match a Golf GTD, it's a crazy little crossover that we all agreed should be on our list. It's definitely no joker in the pack.

Power: *218 bhp*

0–60mph: *7 seconds*

Top Speed: *134 mph*

Price: *£21,645*

Stig Factor:

In the year 20 BC, the fastest thing on the planet was probably a peckish cheetah chasing a gazelle across sub-Saharan Africa.

Spin the clock forward 2,030 years or so and the cheetah has lost that tag to speedy machines like the Huayra BC. This 789-bhp, 6.0-litre twin-turbocharged V12 beast is an upgrade on the 'standard' Huayra, which was already one of the fastest and coolest cars known to mankind. BC is a very suitable name for it too, seeing as it's biblically quick and worshipped by supercar fans. It refers to Benny Caiola, Mr Pagani's first customer, friend and mentor.

 Power: 789 bhp

 0–60mph: 2.8 seconds

Top Speed: 220 mph

Price: £1.89 million

Stig Factor:

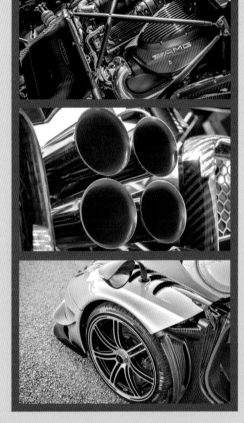

75

75 *Pagani* **Huayra BC**

76 *Pagani* Zonda R

Outrageous looks? Yep. Outrageous speed? You bet. Outrageous price? Of course.

The Zonda R has everything needed to place it firmly in the supercar royal family. If it was any more regal you'd need to perform a curtsey and call it Your Majesty every time it blasted past you. But you would need to stand beside a racetrack in order for it to blast your eardrums and melt your eyebrows, because it's a track-only version of the wonderful Zonda. Take this speed freak on a road and the police could quite possibly shout at you then throw you in prison. A royal pardon would be your only hope.

 Power: 739 bhp

 0–60mph: 3 seconds

 Top Speed: 233 mph

 Price: £1.45 million

 Stig Factor:

77 Peugeot 308 R
HYbrid Concept

The French know a thing or two about good taste. After all, they invented champagne, croissants and Camembert.

They're also responsible for a few tasty hatchbacks over the years, like the Peugeot 205 GTI and the Renault 5 GT. Now the 308 R HYbrid is also on the menu. It's a four-door 308 that's low, wide and has a 268-bhp, 1.6-litre turbo engine supported by two 114-bhp electric motors. It's the fastest road-going Peugeot ever, and if it goes into production it will whet the appetite of many hungry hot-hatch drivers.

 Power: 494 bhp

 0–60mph: 4 seconds

 Top Speed: 155 mph

 Price: £50,000

 Stig Factor:

This book contains lots of petrol-powered 28-litre V12 rockets. That's because diesels are driven by people who spend their lives driving on motorways or in mucky lanes, selling insurance or moving manure.

But in 2012 Peugeot dreamed up the Onyx — a diesel-powered 3.7-litre V8 thing of beauty that somehow summons 600 bhp, with an extra 80 bhp appearing from electric wizardry. It may well be the fastest diesel ever, but Peugeot never released performance figures. We're pretty sure it's quicker than a Mondeo on the M62 or a Defender in the Dales.

 Power: 680 bhp (estimated)

 0–60mph: 3 seconds (estimated)

 Top Speed: 150 mph (estimated)

 Price: Unknown

 Stig Factor:

7日 *Peugeot Onyx Concept*

78

The Pikes Peak International Hill Climb is an annual 12-mile race up a rocky and twisty mountain in Colorado.

The Peugeot 208 T16 was built to blast up that 12-mile, 156-turn route in as little time as possible. Its engine has a bit more power than the standard 208 favoured by nuns and nannies — about 800 bhp more, in fact — and the car weighs just 875 kilograms. The result of all this is that it set a Pikes Peak course record of 8 minutes 13 seconds, knocking a minute and a half off the previous best. It's the most monumental, monstrous and mountainous Peugeot on the planet.

 Power: 875 bhp

 0–60mph: 1.8 seconds

 Top Speed: 151 mph

 Price: Unknown

 Stig Factor:

79

Peugeot
208 T16 Pikes Peak

Porsche *911* GT3 RS

Some car fans questioned whether the 911 GT3 RS would be as quick on the road as on a racetrack.

That's like wondering if it's better to have a billion quid in tenners or fifties. As it turns out, this German racer begs to hit 200 mph on a straight track, and is as happy going sideways as a kid in a Spanish splash park. On public roads it's a happy chap too, and tolerates being driven at 70 mph. Question answered, then. And, for the record, *Top Gear* would prefer the billion quid in £50 notes please, as there's limited space in the back of the GT3 RS to stash it all.

  Power: *493 bhp*

 0–60mph: *3.3 seconds*

 Top Speed: *196 mph*

 Price: *£131,296*

 Stig Factor:

80

Many people are frightened of spiders. That's fair enough, because some are hairier than Chewbacca and scarier than Darth Vader. Fortunately, the Porsche 918 Spyder is not at all hairy and, even though it has more power than two Mitsubishi Evos, it's not all that scary to drive.

It's prettier than a tarantula or a black widow, doesn't kill insects (apart from those splattered on its windscreen) and is nice to the environment with its twin electric motors. We reckon it's the nicest arachnid around, even though it could appear from your kitchen and dart across the living-room carpet at over 200 mph.

 Power: 875 bhp

 0–60mph: 2.6 seconds

 Top Speed: 214 mph

 Price: £704,000

 Stig Factor:

81 Porsche 918 Spyder

The Cayman's had a mixed response from bearded and boring driving-type people. They said it's not as good as the heroic 911, doesn't have enough power and looks a bit pathetic to be a proper Porsche.

Then along came the GT4 to ram those words down their hairy necks. It borrows the 3.8-litre six-cylinder engine from the Carrera S, and on a slightly misty day even looks a bit like its 911 big brother. It's the fastest Cayman too, beating the GTS by a few sneaky miles per hour. The only problem is that its limited production run sold out straight away — probably all bought by bearded boring people.

 Power: 380 bhp

 0–60mph: 4.4 seconds

 Top Speed: 180 mph

 Price: £64,451

 Stig Factor:

Top Gear's favourite cake shop is 155.5 miles away from our office. That means we have a round trip of 311 miles if we want a fondant fancy and flapjack to wash down with our afternoon cuppa.

Luckily, when Porsche announced in 2016 that it would make its Mission E concept a reality, it also confirmed this all-electric supercar could travel 311 miles before the batteries conked out. Which makes it the fastest, coolest and most exciting cake-carrier in the world. Chocolate sponge, anyone?

Power: *592 bhp*

0–60mph: *3.5 seconds*

Top Speed *110 mph (estimated)*

Price: *£100,000 (estimated)*

Stig Factor:

84

84 *Range Rover* Evoque

The Evoque has been a big hit. Wanted by everyone from Premier League footballers to Premier League footballers' wives right down to Premier League footballers' two-year-old children, the baby Rangie has done the business.

For just over £42,000 — or a morning's pay for Mr Rooney — you can pick up the slick 240-bhp, 2.0-litre petrol version and whisk yourself away from Wembley with all the speed and power you're ever likely to need. If that doesn't convince the Chelsea squad to snap one up, remember that David Beckham's wife, Victoria, helped to style the original in 2011. And she knows what she wants — what she really, really wants.

  Power: 240 bhp

 0–60mph: 7.1 seconds

 Top Speed: 135 mph

Price: £42,115

  Stig Factor:

177

If the Evoque is the baby Range Rover, and the Land Rover Vogue's the older brother, is the Sport the difficult middle child? Nope, because the SVR is no spotty-faced, embarrassing sibling, and even has the power to outmuscle its heavier relation.

Weighing 2,335 kilograms, with 22-inch wheels and a mighty 5.0-litre V8 supercharged engine, it's not something you'll easily miss. It's the size of a house, costs about the same as bricks and mortar, and is just as expensive to run. But neither houses nor big brothers can reach 162 mph. This is the firm family favourite.

 Power: 550 bhp

0–60mph: 4.5 seconds

Top Speed: 162 mph

Price: £95,900

Stig Factor:

Renault Alpine
Vision Concept

86

Dreaming up a quick and cool car is almost as much fun as driving one. And when your dream machine is based on an old sports coupé you can be pretty sure it won't turn out to be a nightmare.

That's what the French cheeses at Renault thought in 2016 when they showed *Top Gear* what was keeping them awake at night: their looks-very-fast Alpine Vision, which is based on the A110. (As in the Alpine A110 car that became a 1970s rally fave, not the A110 road that links Woodford to Barnet. No one dreams about that — even if they have been at the French cheese.)

 Power: *250 bhp (estimate)*

 0–60mph: *4.5 seconds (estimate)*

 Top Speed: *135 mph (estimate)*

 Price: *£40,000 (estimate)*

 Stig Factor:

87 Renault *Sport Mégane R.S. 275 Trophy*

Fast cars don't need to be as long as a barge, have a whacking great engine and look at home on a Formula One grid.

That's definitely what Renault believe, because they're quite happy to pull things like rear seats, stereo, air con and windscreen wipers out of their normal, slow and small road cars just to make them quite un-normal and un-slow. This mega-quick 2.0-litre turbocharged Mégane has been through that weight-saving process and come out with a belly full of power, torque and speed. The only thing that's long about this car is its name.

 Power: 271 bhp

 0–60mph: 6 seconds

 Top Speed: 158 mph

 Price: £28,930

 Stig Factor:

The Wraith is meant to be the 'small and sporty' version of the smallest Roller, the Ghost. The only thing is that the Ghost is still bigger than an already-big BMW 7 Series, and so is its little offshoot.

So the Wraith is not small at all. We're happy to confirm, however, that it is still sporty, with a 6.6-litre V12 twin-turbocharged unit under its sweeping bonnet,

and a top speed that's been limited to 155 mph. We suspect that's just in case you went bonkers with the accelerator and made your VIP passengers feel a bit dizzy all the way back there on the rear seats.

 Power: *624 bhp*

 0–60mph: *4.4 seconds*

 Top Speed: *155 mph*

 Price: *£229,128*

 Stig Factor:

Rolls-Royce *Wraith*

The Volkswagen Group owns a stack of heavyweight motoring brands, such as Bentley, Bugatti, Lamborghini and Porsche. The SEAT Leon, then, might feel a bit narked to be part of the VW family but put together with lightweight pieces pinched from a Golf, an Audi A3 and a Škoda Octavia.

But it's not all sad news, as at least the CUPRA's parts were prised from speedy models like the S3 and Golf GTs. This cut-and-paste job means the Cupra has ended up with a respectable 286 bhp and sub-six seconds to 60 mph. Shame _it_ couldn't swipe the scissor doors and V12 from a Lambo.

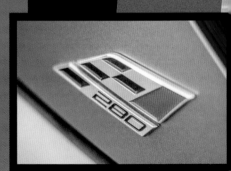

Power: 286 bhp

0–60mph: 5.6 seconds

Top Speed: 155 mph

Price: £28,765

Stig Factor: 👽👽👽

09 SEAT Leon CUPRA

American motors such as the Mustang are often called muscle cars. In the case of the Mustang, this is because they're big and brutish, with more power than they can cope with.

Also, it can get a bit sweaty and hot under the collar if it's worked too hard, requiring a rest in the shade to avoid a complete breakdown. We're pleased to say the 2015 GT350R, after a once-over from specialist tuner Shelby, has no such health issues, and flexes

both arms to administer 526 bhp from its 5.2-litre V8. This 'Stang is fast enough and practical enough to be used for everyday driving, even if it is more at home in Texas than Toys R Us.

Power: 526 bhp

0-60mph: 4 seconds

Top Speed: 175 mph

Price: £58,000

Stig Factor:

91 *Subaru* **WRX STI S207**

Subaru Imprezas are very fast, very noisy and very easy to spot on UK roads. That's because they're often followed by a police car with sirens screaming and lights flashing like a disco.

Officers seem very interested in asking Scooby drivers how fast they thought they were going back there. But the British bobby need not worry about catching up with the WRX STI S207 model, as all 400 examples are only for sale in Japan.

So this bright yellow, rally-inspired rocket blaster will be a rare sight on these shores — though listen carefully and you'll probably hear one smoking its tyres 6,000 miles away in Tokyo.

 Power: 325 bhp

 0–60mph: 5 seconds (estimate)

 Top Speed: 160 mph (estimate)

 Price: Only for sale in Japan

 Stig Factor:

Tesla *Model S P90D*

92

For pure petrolheads, the fact that one of the fastest and most powerful cars in this book is powered by an electric motor and not fossil fuels won't go down well.

But this Tesla shoots down the motorway, reaching 70 mph in a ferocious 4.1 seconds.

To have such awesome acceleration, you need to pay Tesla an extra £8,700 to have a button in the control menu marked Ludicrous Speed. This may sound like the name of an American rapper, but we're not joking — flick that switch and be prepared to travel faster than the speed of light. Any petrolhead would nod to that.

 Power: 762 bhp

 0–60mph: 3.2 seconds

 Top Speed: 155 mph

 Price: £81,900

 Stig Factor:

93

You might think a Touring Disco involves a battered Transit turning up at a social-club car park, flinging open its doors and blasting out One Direction songs from six-foot speakers.

Well it does in the UK, but in Italy it refers to cool coachbuilders Touring taking an already stunning Alfa Romeo 8C Spider and making it even more stunning. They changed the panels, doorframes and overall look of the Alfa to end up with the Disco Volante — but luckily the 4.7-litre V8 engine stays in place. That means there's only one direction this new car moves, and that's forward — extremely quickly.

 Power: *444 bhp*

 0–60mph: *4.5 seconds*

 Top Speed: *181 mph*

 Price: *£250,000+ (estimate)*

 Stig Factor:

Toyota's small sports coupé was only tweaked a little bit for its 2016 update, meaning the 2012 original must have been a pretty decent effort in the first place.

Indeed it was. With skinny tyres, rear-wheel drive and a 2.0-litre flat-4 stashed in the front, the GT86 is up there fighting with the Peugeot RCZ, MINI Coupé and VW Scirocco for the title of lightweight champ. It's *Top*

Gear's fave by a long way and just goes to show what can be achieved if you keep things simple and fun. A proper little star.

 Power: *202 bhp*

 0–60mph: *7.6 seconds*

 Top Speed: *140 mph*

 Price: *£25,000*

 Stig Factor:

94

There's no doubt this Spanish supercar is super quick. Put 720 bhp in something that weighs less than a goldfish and it's going to hurry along at epic speeds.

But the problem with this F1-inspired, futuristic-looking machine is that no one knows what it is. Owners will spend so long telling people that it's not a Zonda, not a Lambo and not a KTM that they'll never get to work on time. And they'll need to hold on to their jobs just to have the cash to keep this thing going. You could buy a Spanish villa for less than the Tramontana R.

 Power: *720 bhp*

 0–60mph: *3.6 seconds*

 Top Speed: *203 mph*

 Price: *£385,000*

 Stig Factor: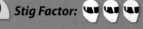

95 *Tramontana R*

We could tell you all about the limited-slip diff, the HiPer Strut front suspension or the FlexRide adaptive dampers that mark this Astra out from a run-of-the-mill 1.6-litre diesel. But your eyes would glaze over and tears (of boredom) would soon stream down your face.

So, instead, we'll say that the Stig simply loves this hot hatch and the fun he has with it on the *Top Gear* track. It's not often that words like 'sophisticated', 'clever' and 'lovely' are used to describe a Vauxhall, but they describe this 2.0-litre turbo to a tee. Plus, they're much easier to understand than 'electro-hydraulic steering'.

 Power: *280 bhp*

 0–60mph: *5.9 seconds*

 Top Speed: *155 mph*

 Price: *£27,215*

 Stig Factor:

There's no space in this book for the legendary Golf GTI. Boo! But there is space for the Golf R. Result! For those of you unfamiliar with the 2.0-litre turbocharged R – and if that's you, why on Earth are you reading this book? Boo! – it's a much faster, much more powerful and much crazier version of the GTI.

Fitted with the paddle-shift double-clutch gearbox, it will make you feel like a proper racing driver as you pop to the post office and back. Make sure you 'accidentally' forget to buy your stamps though, just so you have the pleasure of taking the trip all over again.

Power: *297 bhp*

0–60mph: *4.9 seconds*

Top Speed: *155 mph*

Price: *£31,120*

Stig Factor: 🏁🏁🏁🏁

97

98 *Volkswagen XL1*

98

In the 1960s there was a TV cartoon called *The Jetsons*. Set in a space-age world, George Jetson drove and flew a strange dome-shaped vehicle at hyper speeds.

Zoom forward 50 years and it seemed VW had created George's car for real when they released the XL1. Not quite able to run on moon dust, it has an 800-cc diesel engine and an electric motor to whip up 68 bhp. This means it's not fast at all on the road, but it does look ultra fast, has scissor doors, enclosed rear wheels and sits lower than a Porsche Boxster. We like it, you like it, and we're pretty sure George Jetson would have liked it too.

 Power: 68 bhp

 0–60mph 12.7 seconds

 Top Speed: 99 mph

 Price: £100,000+

 Stig Factor:

201

None of you will cry because the Volvo S60, S80 and V40 do not appear in this book. A few of you may have blubbed if the beastly blue Volvo C30 Polestar hatchback you're looking at hadn't showed up, though.

Based on the riotous C30 rally car, its 2.5-litre turbo was taken from a Focus RS and modified to within an inch of its life to spew out 400 bhp. With a beefy bodykit, double-decker rear spoiler and 19-inch alloys, it was the fastest road-going Volvo when performance company Polestar revealed it in 2010. It never made the showrooms though, which made *Top Gear* blub a little.

 Power: *400 bhp*

 0–60mph: *4.6 seconds*

 Top Speed: *140 mph (estimate)*

 Price: *Not for sale*

 Stig Factor:

99 *Volvo C30*
Polestar Concept

100 *Zenos E10*

In an A to Z of speedy cars, the Zenos E10 quite rightly holds its head up against other, ahem, speedsters like the Citroën ZX and the Vauxhall Zafira.

Built by a bunch of blokes who used to work at Lotus and Caterham, and therefore know a thing or two about low-slung racers, it extracts every bit of power possible from its Ford Focus ST 2.0-litre turbo engine. And, because it weighs 600 kilograms less than a Focus, the Zenos can zoom from zero to 60 mph quicker than an Audi R8 V10. It's a doddle to drive as well — in fact it's as easy as ABC.

 Power: *247 bhp*

 0–60mph: *4 seconds*

 Top Speed: *145 mph*

 Price: *£29,995*

 Stig Factor:

E10S GO

100